GET UNTAMED

I AM ....

....

month/year

We must feel all of our feelings.
We must be still and know.
We must dare to imagine.
And we must always
be willing to let burn
what isn't true enough anymore
in order to build the new.
Again and again forever.
These things are hard.
But we can do hard things.
Because when we do,
we finally become alive.

The moment I met my wife, Abby, my entire being said: *There She Is.*

It was like the voice that was becoming clearer and louder ever since I got sober fifteen years earlier had finally shouted.

When I met Abby, it was just weeks before *Love Warrior*—my memoir about the healing of my marriage after my husband's infidelities; the book that Oprah had chosen for her Book Club, and which was being touted as "An Epic Marriage Redemption Story"—was to be released.

When I met Abby, it was bad timing.

But when I met Abby, I knew that I was meant to love her and be loved by her. I knew in the way we pretend not to know terribly inconvenient, scary, true things. I knew like I knew when I looked down at that positive pregnancy test fifteen years earlier—hungover, addicted, and alone—that I was meant to become a mother to Chase, my first baby. I knew like I knew when I began typing and saw my hidden, wild self appear in black letters on a blank white screen that I was made to be a writer.

I knew I was meant to be with Abby. I just knew.

My friends pointed to my kids and said: *This will destroy them.*

My colleagues pointed to my career: *This will destroy all that you've built.*

Oh my God. They all said: *You will lose everything!*

And I shook as I decided: *Okay, then. I guess I must lose this life to find my next one.*

I left my husband and lost my marriage. My kids lost the idea that their parents could or would protect them from pain. I lost readers and speaking events. Christian leaders wrote scathing pieces excommunicating me, and I lost a belonging I'd sometimes felt inside of church.

It was all hard. But it was finally the right kind of hard. I lost and lost and lost. But I also found. For the first time, I found integrity, freedom, and comfort inside my sexuality, family, faith, and skin.

I'm not saying the secret to happiness is leaving your partner for an Olympian. I don't even believe in happily ever after. My aim is not to feel happy, it's to feel everything. I don't need happy, I need alive. In order to finally come to life, I had to trust myself for the first time. I had to trade acceptance for freedom and love. I had to abandon everyone else's expectations of me so I could stop abandoning myself. I had to quit pleasing to start living.

When Abby told my mother that she was going to propose to me, my mother cried and said, "I have not seen my daughter this alive since she was ten years old."

This alive.

When we're young, we're all feelings, imagination, and intuition. We don't have two selves yet. We're integrated. But somewhere between the ages of seven and twelve we begin to internalize our social conditioning. We learn that we are not good enough, beautiful enough, cool enough, safe enough, worthy enough as we are. We see all the ways that our real selves are not fit for public consumption. So we slowly surrender our true, wild selves to become who our families, peers, religions, and cultures tell us we should be. We abandon who we are to become who the world wants us to be. We are tamed by shame. We split in two: our tender inside self and our representative self, the one we send out into the world. Over time, we forget our wild self—she's buried beneath the world's ideals and expectations.

But every once in a while, we still hear from her, don't we? Each time we feel an ache of discontent or a spark of aliveness—that's her, trying to get our attention, insisting to us that good enough is not good enough, waiting for us to return to her, to set her free. When we quit ignoring her, we resurrect. We come alive, to the self and life we were meant for before we were tamed by shame. That's what happened when I allowed myself to love and be loved by Abby. That is what my mom was seeing in my eyes: me again.

There She Is. It was not about seeing Abby. It was about finally seeing Me. Resurrected. Alive.

But I almost missed all of this. At first, I decided to let Abby go, to bury my wild self again and to return to my broken marriage. I decided this because I was so desperate to be a "good" mother to my three children. I'd been conditioned to believe that a good mother never hurts her children, and she certainly doesn't break up her family.

One day, I told my therapist about Abby. I'd been working with this therapist for years, so she knew the struggle of my marriage. She knew about the infidelities. She knew it all. She listened to me and then she said: "Glennon. This 'love' for Abby is not real. It's a distraction. You are a mother, and you have responsibilities."

Later that night, I was sitting behind my daughter Tish, in front of a mirror, braiding her hair. And I had this life-saving thought:

I am staying in this marriage for her, but would I want this marriage for her?

And if I would not want this broken marriage for my baby girl, then why am I modeling bad love and calling that good parenting?

All my life I'd received the memo that a good mother is a martyr, that our duty is to slowly die for our children—to bury our dreams, passion, ambition, emotion, and humanity and to call that love. What a burden to pass down to our children. To give our children this legacy—that love means disappearing and dying instead of emerging fully and living—is to lay upon our babies a legacy that is a lie. This is why Carl Jung said that the greatest burden a child can bear is the unlived life of a parent.

I decided to quit showing my children how to slowly die and instead show them how to bravely live. I became their model, not their martyr. My children didn't need me to save them, they needed to watch their mother save herself. My therapist was right: *I am a mother and I have responsibilities*—including living the life I want my babies to believe they deserve and refusing to settle for any life, relationship, community, or world less beautiful than the one I'd want for them. I felt myself coming to life.

So, one by one, I began examining the other cultural memos I wanted to let burn. I decided to live as though I had never received any of my culture's memos. I wanted to begin living not in obedience to or rebellion against the world's expectations (rebellion is as much a cage as obedience is) but from my own emotions, intuition, and imagination. I wanted to create a life, marriage, family, career, and spirituality that I recognized as my own. To live by design instead of default. To live from the inside out. To quit asking people for directions to places they've never been. We are all pioneers, after all.

In this journal, we'll walk step-by-step through that process. We will unearth the culturally constructed ideals that control how we live, interact, and feel, and we will decide what we want to stay and what we'll let burn as we rewrite our own memos to live by. We'll explore how to stop fearing pain and ecstasy—how to feel it all and use it all. We'll remember how to hear from our intuition again and how to live by its wisdom. We'll imagine and begin to build truer, more beautiful lives for ourselves and a more equitable world for us all.

Readers of *Untamed* have written me to share so many of their imaginings for truer, more beautiful lives. I marvel at how wildly different they all are. It's proof that our lives were never meant to be cookie-cutter, culturally constructed carbon copies of some ideal. There is no one way to live, love, raise children, arrange a family, run a school, a community, a nation. The norms were created by somebody, and each of us is somebody. We can make our own normal. We can throw out all the rules and write our own.

We'll do this by working through seven sections:

- **UNEARTH YOUR BELIEFS**
- **FEEL IT ALL, USE IT ALL**
- **BE STILL AND KNOW**
- **DARE TO IMAGINE**
- **TRUST YOURSELF**
- **LET IT BURN**
- **BUILD THE NEW**

We'll do this by asking ourselves: *Is my life, are my relationships, and is my world the truest, most beautiful I can imagine?* If they are not, and we dare to admit they are not, we will decide if we have the guts, the right, perhaps even the duty, to let burn that which is not true and beautiful enough and get started building what is.

Stay open as you work through these pages. Give yourself time to breathe, think, let rise what's inside of you. You don't need to act yet, so don't hold back. Just write and sketch it all out. An architect always puts her ideas on paper before she begins to build, because the truest, most beautiful anything must often come to life one dimension at a time. Write the words you must write. Do not be afraid. Remember: You're a goddamn cheetah. Eventually, you will discover that imagination is not where we go to escape reality but to remember it, and what you create in this journal are not just your fantasies but the original blueprints of your truest, most beautiful life.

As you bring these pages—and yourself—to life, I hope you will look with awe and think to yourself: *There She Is.*

Love, Solidarity, and Relentless Hope,

Glennon

Two summers ago, my wife and I took our daughters to the zoo. As we walked the grounds, we saw a sign advertising the Cheetah Run. We found a viewing spot along the route.

A peppy zookeeper appeared, and she held the leash of a Labrador retriever.

She began, "Welcome, everybody! You are about to meet our resident cheetah, Tabitha. Do you think this is Tabitha?"

"Nooooo!" the kids yelled.

"This sweet Labrador is Minnie, Tabitha's best friend. We introduced them when Tabitha was a baby, and we raised Minnie alongside Tabitha to help tame her. Whatever Minnie does, Tabitha wants to do."

The zookeeper motioned toward a parked jeep with a pink stuffed bunny tied to the tailgate.

"Minnie loves to chase this bunny! So first, Minnie will do the Cheetah Run while Tabitha watches. Then we'll count down, I'll open Tabitha's cage, and she'll take off."

The zookeeper signaled to the jeep, and it raced off. She released Minnie's leash, and we all watched the Lab joyfully chase that dirty pink bunny.

Finally, it was time for Tabitha's big moment. The zookeeper opened her cage door, and the bunny took off again. Tabitha bolted out, crossed the finish line within seconds, and the crowd broke into applause.

I didn't clap, though. I felt queasy. The taming of Tabitha felt . . . familiar.

I watched Tabitha and thought: *Day after day this wild animal chases dirty pink bunnies down the well-worn path they've cleared for her. Never catching that damn bunny, settling instead for a store-bought steak and the approval of strangers. Obeying every command, just like Minnie, the Lab she's been trained to believe she is. Unaware that if she remembered her wildness—just for a moment—she could tear those zookeepers to shreds.*

A young girl raised her hand and asked, "Isn't Tabitha sad? Doesn't she miss the wild?"

The zookeeper smiled and said, "No. Tabitha was born here. She doesn't know any different. This is a good life for Tabitha."

While the zookeeper shared facts about cheetahs born in captivity, my older daughter, Tish, nudged me and pointed to Tabitha. There, in that field, Tabitha's posture had changed. Her head was high, and she was stalking the periphery, tracing the boundaries the fence created, back and forth, like she was remembering something. She looked regal. And a little scary.

Tish whispered to me, "Mommy. She turned wild again."

I looked at Tabitha. I wished I could ask her, "What's happening inside you right now?"

I knew she'd say, "Something's off about my life. I feel restless and frustrated. I have this hunch that everything was supposed to be more beautiful than this."

Then she'd look back at the cage, the only home she's ever known. She'd look at the zookeepers, the spectators, and her panting, begging best friend, the Lab.

She'd sigh and say, "I should be grateful. I have a good enough life here. It's crazy to long for what doesn't even exist."

I'd say:

Tabitha. You are not crazy.
You are a goddamn cheetah.

The idea of a gender binary is something I've begun to let burn since I wrote *Untamed*. It doesn't feel true enough to me anymore to restrict our language to labels like boy and girl or man and woman. For some people, these labels are just right—even empowering—but for others, like me, they aren't sufficient to describe our whole self. I haven't yet found the words to write myself a new memo about gender. I'm deconstructing an old understanding without having the language to construct a new one yet. I created *Get Untamed* during this in-between time.

In this journal, I use words like *boy* and *girl, man* and *woman, she, he, her,* and *him.* I hope that even as I use these labels, the exercises in these pages might help us imagine fuller, truer, more beautiful ways to describe who we are.

Love,

G

"I wanted to be a
good girl, so I surrendered
to my cages. I chose
a personality, a body,
a faith, and a sexuality
so tiny I had to hold
my breath to fit
myself inside."

UN—EARTH YOUR BELIEFS

"We are like computers, and our beliefs are the software with which we're programmed. Often our beliefs are programmed into us without our knowledge by our culture, community, religion, and family. Even though we don't choose those subconscious programs, they run our lives. They control our decisions, perspectives, feelings, and interactions, so they determine our destiny. What we believe, we become. There is nothing more important than unearthing what we really believe to be true about ourselves and our world."

Let's begin by unearthing ideals and expectations that you grew up with. What were you taught to believe makes a good daughter/child?

a Good Daughter / Child...

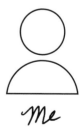

Me

"When I found myself pregnant with Chase, I quit drinking, drugging, and purging. I thought it might be my last chance to stop being bad and start being good. I married Chase's father, and I learned to cook and clean and fake orgasms. I was a good wife."

What have you been conditioned to believe makes a good wife/partner?

a Good Wife / Partner ...

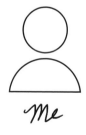

Me

"I am not a good friend. I have never been capable of or willing to commit to the maintenance that the rules of friendship dictate. I cannot remember birthdays. I do not want to meet for coffee. I will not host the baby shower. I won't text back because it's an eternal game of ping-pong, the texting. It never ends. I inevitably disappoint friends, so after enough of that, I decided I would stop trying. I don't want to live in constant debt. This is okay with me. I have a sister and children and a dog. One cannot have it all."

What were you trained to believe makes a good friend?

a Good Friend...

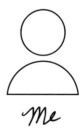

me

"Mothers have martyred themselves in their children's names since the beginning of time. We have been trained to prove our love by ceasing to exist. What a terrible burden for children to bear—to become the reason their mother stopped living. To know that their mother refused to live and used them as the reason. To learn that if they choose to have children, one day this will be their fate, too."

What did your family, culture, and world teach you to believe about what makes a good mother?

a Good Mother...

Me

"The thing that gets me thinking and questioning most deeply is a leader who warns me not to think or question."

What have you been conditioned to believe makes a good leader?

A Good Leader...

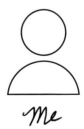

Me

What were you taught to believe about gender? How have you been conditioned to believe that good girls behave? How have you been trained to believe real boys behave?

What were you raised to believe about sexuality? What types of people were you taught to love? How were you taught to express or repress that love?

"It struck me that in every family, culture, religion, ideas of right and wrong are the hot cattle prods, the barking sheepdogs that keep the masses in the herd. They are the bars that keep us caged."

What were you taught to believe about faith and religion?

What did your culture hold up as ideals for you to strive for?

....

....

....

....

....

....

....

....

....

....

....

....

....

As a white woman, I was conditioned to believe that the ideal woman is pleasant,
accommodating, polite, silent, and, thus, complicit with abuse of power. I have been trained
to abandon myself instead of rocking the boat; to stay small in body, ambition, and voice.
The role I was given to play was this: Accept the benefits of my proximity to power without
demanding any real power or speaking truth to power.

GLENNON

Do any of these roles—good daughter, good wife, good friend, good mother, good leader, ideal person—feel like cages? How and why?

"Ten is when we learn how to be good girls and real boys.
Ten is when children begin to hide who they are in order
to become what the world expects them to be.
Right around ten is when we begin to internalize our formal
training. Ten is when we begin to be tamed by shame.
Ten is when the world sat me down, told me to be quiet,
and pointed toward my cages:
These are the feelings you are allowed to express.
This is how a woman should act.
This is the body you must strive for.
These are the things you will believe.
These are the people you can love.
Those are the people you should fear.
This is the kind of life you are supposed to want.
Make yourself fit. You'll be uncomfortable at first,
but don't worry—eventually you'll forget you're caged.
Soon this will just feel like: life."

What parts of your original wild self were you taught to be ashamed of?

What kind of support did your younger self need that you did not have?

If you could tell your younger self one thing, what would it be?

That support you needed when you were younger—do you get it now? If not, how could you begin to build it?

"When I was a child, I felt what I needed to feel and I followed my gut and I planned only from my imagination. I was wild until I was tamed by shame. Until I started hiding and numbing my feelings for fear of being too much. Until I started deferring to others' advice instead of trusting my own intuition. Until I became convinced that my imagination was ridiculous and my desires were selfish. Until I surrendered myself to the cages of others' expectations, cultural mandates, and institutional allegiances. Until I buried who I was in order to become what I should be. I lost myself when I learned how to please."

When you were a child, what types of things did you love to do?

1

2

3

4

5

GET UNTAMED

"Ask a woman who she is, and she'll tell you who she loves, who she serves, and what she does. *I am a mother, a wife, a sister, a friend, a career woman.* The fact that we define ourselves by our roles is what keeps the world spinning. It's also what makes us untethered and afraid. If a woman defines herself as a wife, what happens if her partner leaves? If a woman defines herself as a mother, what happens when the kids leave for college? If a woman defines herself as a career woman, what happens when the company folds? *Who we are* is perpetually being taken from us, so we live in fear instead of peace. That is why so many women feel invisible."

Describe how you spend your time in an average week. How much of your time is spent feeding your soul? How much time is spent playing your roles?

What cage are you most desperate to break out of? Why?

....

....

....

....

....

....

....

....

....

....

....

....

....

....

....

....

I've found it damn near impossible to deprogram myself from the deadly memo that women should deny our hunger and stay small in body. I still struggle mightily with food and body issues. This cage feels like my final frontier.

GLENNON

"Then I built a life of my own. I did it by
resurrecting the very parts of me I was
trained to mistrust, hide, and abandon in
order to keep others comfortable:

My emotions
My intuition
My imagination
My courage.

Those are the keys to freedom.
Those are who we are.
Will we be brave enough to unlock ourselves?
Will we be brave enough to set ourselves free?
Will we finally step out of our cages
and say to ourselves, to our people,
and to the world: Here I Am."

What do you want more than anything in the world?

What is keeping you from getting it?

I reach deeply into the rich soil beneath me,
made up of every girl and woman I've ever been,
every face I've loved, every love I've lost, every
place I've been, every conversation I've had,
everything, everything, crumbling and mixing
and decomposing underneath. Nothing wasted.

My entire past there, holding me up and feeding me now. I am as ancient as the earth I'm planted in and as new as my tiniest bloom. I am strong, singular, alive. Still growing. I have everything I need, beneath me, above me, inside me.

"Being fully human
is not about
feeling happy,
it's about feeling
everything."

FEEL IT ALL, USE IT ALL

How do you feel right now?

How do you *want* to feel?

GET UNTAMED

As a child, what feelings were you taught not to feel or express?

"It's okay to feel all of the stuff you're feeling. You're just becoming human again. You're not doing life wrong; you're doing it right. If there's any secret you're missing, it's that doing it right is just really hard. Feeling all your feelings is hard, but that's what they're for. Feelings are for feeling. All of them. Even the hard ones. The secret is that you're doing it right, and that doing it right hurts sometimes."

As an adult, what feelings are most difficult for you to feel or express?

"Everything I need to become
the woman I'm meant to be next
is inside my hard feelings of now.
Life is alchemy, and emotions are
the fire that turns me to gold.
I will continue to become only if
I resist extinguishing myself a
million times a day. If I do resist—
if I can sit in the fire of my own
feelings—I will keep becoming."

What are you afraid will happen if you allow yourself to Feel It All?

I used to believe that my feelings were a manhole in the road. If I fell in, I'd never get back out. So my job each day was to circle the manhole but never ever slip in. I thought if I felt it all, it would kill me.

GLENNON

FEEL IT ALL, USE IT ALL

"Easy buttons are the things
that appear in front of us
that we want to reach for
because they temporarily take us
out of our feelings, pain, and stress.
They do not work in the long run,
because what they actually do
is help us abandon ourselves.
You know you've hit an easy
button when, afterward, you feel
more lost in the woods than you
did before you hit it."

"It has taken me forty years to decide that when I feel bad, I want to do something that makes me feel better instead of worse. I keep a handwritten poster in my office titled 'Easy Buttons and Reset Buttons.' On the left are all the things I do to abandon myself. On the right are my reset buttons, the things I can do to make staying with myself a little more possible."

EASY BUTTONS	RESET BUTTONS
- Boozing	- Drink a glass of water
- Bingeing	- Take a walk
- Shopping	- Take a bath
- Snarking	- Practice yoga
- Comparing	- Meditate
- Reading mean reviews	- Go to the beach and watch the waves
- Inhaling loads of sugar and passing out	- Play with my dog
	- Hug my wife and kids
	- Hide the phone

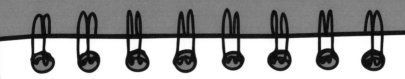

MY EASY BUTTONS | MY RESET BUTTONS

"When I got sober, I learned that hard feelings are doorbells that interrupt me, send me into a panic, and then leave me with an exciting package. Sobriety is a decision to stop numbing and blaming away hard feelings and to start answering the door. So when I quit drinking, I began allowing my feelings to disturb me. This was scary, because I had always assumed that my feelings were so big and powerful that they would stay forever and eventually kill me. But my hard feelings did not stay forever, and they did not kill me. Instead, they came and went, and afterward I was left with something I didn't have before. That something was self-knowledge. As I practiced allowing my hard feelings to come and stay as long as they needed to, I got to know myself. The reward for enduring hard feelings was finding my potential, my purpose, and my people."

"I numbed myself with food and booze trying to control my anger. When I quit, I learned that my anger never meant that there was something wrong with me. It meant that there was something wrong. Out there. Something I might have the power to change. I stopped being a quiet peacekeeper and started being a loud peacemaker."

ANGER

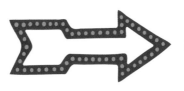
WHAT YOU'RE MEANT TO CHANGE

What makes you angry about yourself?

What makes you angry about your relationships?

What makes you angry about the world?

"Anger delivers important information about where one of our boundaries has been crossed. When we answer the door and accept that delivery, we begin to know ourselves better. When we restore the boundary that was violated, we honor ourselves."

Abby will lie down on our couch and watch zombie shows in the middle of the day. When she does this, I get agitated, then angry, because she is relaxing at me. I start tidying loudly and aggressively in the couch's vicinity. She hears my violent tidying and asks, "What's wrong?" I say, "Nothing" with a tone that suggests "Something." This dance plays out again and again: Abby relaxing on the couch and me getting angry about it, and Abby getting angry that I'm getting angry.

One day I walked into our family room and saw Abby jump off the couch and begin straightening pillows, trying to look busy and productive for my sake. I stopped in my tracks and stared at her while a memory from childhood floated into my mind. When I was young, if I was at home relaxing on the couch and I heard my parents' car pull up in the driveway, I'd panic, jump off the couch, and try to look busy before they opened the door. Exactly like I'd just seen Abby do.

That's when I stopped looking at Abby and thinking: *What is my anger telling me about her?* And started asking: *What is my anger telling me about me?* My anger was delivering a package with one of my root beliefs in it— a belief that was programmed into me during childhood: Resting is laziness, and laziness is disrespect. Worthiness and goodness are earned with hustle.

When Abby rested right in front of me—outside family-designated and approved resting times—she was challenging that root belief. But unlike my root belief about honesty and fidelity, I didn't like this one. It didn't feel true to me. Because when I looked at Abby relaxing, my anger was almost a bitter yearning.

Must be nice.

Must be nice to rest in the middle of the damn day.

Must be nice to rest and still feel worthy.

I want to be able to rest and still feel worthy, too.

I didn't want to change Abby. I wanted to change my belief about worthiness.

Anger rings our bell and delivers one of our root beliefs. This is good information, but the next part is more than informative, it's transformational: All of the beliefs that anger delivers come with a return label.

I looked hard at the root belief about worthiness that my anger at Abby had delivered to me. I thought: *No. I don't want to keep this one. It was inherited by me, not created by me. I have outgrown it. It is no longer my truest, most beautiful belief about worthiness. I know better than this belief. It's harsh, and it's hurting me and my marriage. I don't want to pass this one down to my kids. But I don't want to return it, either. I want to exchange it for this amended one:*

Hard work is important. So are play and nonproductivity. My worth is tied not to my productivity but to my existence. I am worthy of rest.

Changing my root belief about worthiness has changed my life. I sleep a little bit later. I schedule in time for reading and walks and yoga, and sometimes (on the weekend), I even watch a TV show in the middle of the day. It's heavenly. It's also an ongoing process: Still, when I see Abby relaxing, my knee-jerk reaction is annoyance. But then I check myself. I think: *Why am I activated here? Oh, yes, that old belief. Oh, wait, never mind. I've exchanged that one.* And when Abby asks, "What's wrong?" I can say, "Nothing, honey" and mean it, mostly.

What might your anger be trying to reveal to you about your boundaries and beliefs?

Are there beliefs you would like to change or boundaries you would like to set?

"We're only envious of those already doing what we were made to do. Envy is a giant, flashing arrow pointing us toward what to do next."

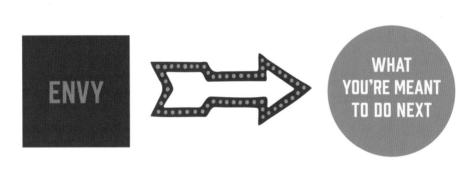

Of what and whom are you envious?

During my decade as a drunk, I could not read beautifully written books. Partly because all the words were quite blurry, but also because something about reading profound words that another woman had written felt like looking straight at the sun: It burned, hurt, and made me look away. The burning and hurting were envy.

Back then, I didn't know my job was to answer the door and let envy make its delivery. So I did everything I could do to ignore the knocking. I snarked, dismissed, and criticized. I rolled my eyes and insisted I didn't like their writing anyway. These things were easier than trying. They were less vulnerable than trying. It felt safer to criticize someone else for trying than to try myself. But ignoring envy's knock didn't make it go away.

Thankfully, envy was persistent. Over time, I started getting curious about what was on the other side. I asked myself: *What if this envy is not a problem but information? What if this envy is trying to deliver me to myself?* Eventually it became clear to me that the only way to make envy stop burning was to answer the door and accept its delivery. Instead of refusing to feel it, I decided to try to feel it all the way through.

I sat with it. I interrogated it. I asked: *Why would it be that I am envious of these particular women—writers and speakers?*

I felt envious because somewhere deep I knew a healthier, braver version of me could do that. Was made to do that. Was made to write. And I wasn't writing. And there is not much that's more painful than watching someone else doing something you know you could do if you were brave enough to try. I suspect we are only envious of folks who are doing what we were made to do. I suspect that envy burns to get us to do something with what we've been given.

What does your envy tell you about what you are meant to do next?

FEEL IT ALL, USE IT ALL

"Heartbreak is not something to be avoided; it's something to pursue. Heartbreak is one of the greatest clues of our lives. What breaks your heart? Is it racial injustice? Bullying? Animal cruelty? Hunger? What is it that affects you so deeply that whenever you encounter it, you feel the need to look away? Look there. Where is the pain in the world that you just cannot stand? Stand there. The thing that breaks your heart is the very thing you were born to help heal. Every world changer's work begins with a broken heart."

 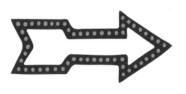

"Heartbreak delivers your purpose. If you are brave enough to accept that delivery and seek out the people doing that particular world-changing work, you find your people. There is no bond like the bond that is forged among people who are united in the same world-healing work. Despair says, *The heartbreak is too overwhelming. I am too sad and too small, and the world is too big. I cannot do it all, so I will do nothing.* Courage says, *I will not let the fact that I cannot do everything keep me from doing what I can.* We all want purpose and connection. Tell me what breaks your heart, and I'll point you toward both."

What breaks your heart about your life, your relationships, your community, your nation, the world?

What might your heartbreak reveal to you about your purpose?

If you were to allow your heartbreak to propel you toward one simple action today—what might that action be?

....

....

....

....

....

....

....

....

....

....

....

....

....

....

....

....

....

....

"The change that happens
to people who really sit in their pain—
whether it's a sliver of envy lasting
an hour or a canyon of grief lasting
decades—it's revolutionary. When
that kind of transformation happens,
it becomes impossible to fit into
your old conversations or relationships
or patterns or thoughts or life anymore.
There is no going back.
We have to let ourselves become
completely, utterly, new."

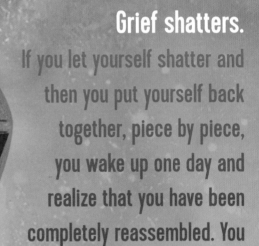

Grief shatters.
If you let yourself shatter and then you put yourself back together, piece by piece, you wake up one day and realize that you have been completely reassembled. You are whole again and strong, but you are suddenly a new shape, a new size.

Grief is a cocoon from which we emerge new.

When in your life have you experienced grief? How did it shatter you?

FEEL IT ALL, USE IT ALL

"Grief is love's souvenir. It's our proof that we once loved. Grief is the receipt we wave in the air that says to the world: *Look! Love was once mine. I loved well. Here is my proof that I paid the price.*"

"Sometimes to live again, we have to let ourselves die completely. We have to let ourselves become completely, utterly, new. When grief rings: Surrender. There is nothing else to do. The delivery is utter transformation."

How has grief transformed you? In what ways did you emerge new?

"When I got pregnant and sober, I was so afraid that actually feeling all of the feelings I'd been numbing for so long would kill me. I needed to practice feeling in manageable bits. Each night after work, I'd lie in bed and play one Indigo Girls song. Nothing made me feel more deeply and widely than the music and poetry of Amy and Emily. I'd lie there, for one song, and listen, and feel, and cry."

G'S FEEL IT ALL PLAYLIST

"Let It Ring" *by Amy Ray*

"Virginia Woolf" *by The Indigo Girls*

"Medicine" *by Daughter*

"Talkin' Bout a Revolution" *by Tracy Chapman*

"Halo" *by Beyoncé*

"Godspeed" *by The Chicks*

"I Am Here" *by P!nk*

"Livin' on a Prayer" *by Bon Jovi*

"Landslide" *by Fleetwood Mac*

"The House That Built Me" *by Miranda Lambert*

"Let It Ring" reminds me of my lifelong complicated relationship with religion. It makes me feel fiery, rebellious, and powerful.

"Virginia Woolf" reminds me of finding the writing of other women for the first time. It makes me feel grateful that I found the lifeboats of books and the blank page.

"Medicine" reminds me of being lost inside the whale of addiction. It makes me feel sad for and proud of my younger self.

"Talkin' Bout a Revolution" reminds me of every justice march, protest, or action I've ever been part of or watched others unleash. It makes me feel hopeful and determined.

"Halo" reminds me of falling in love with Abby. It makes me feel butterflies and nostalgia for those early days of in-love insanity.

"Godspeed" reminds me of when Chase was little. Now he's off to college. It makes me feel deeply achy.

"I Am Here" reminds me of the need to fight religious and gender cages and to claim my full humanity. It makes me feel free and strong and wild.

"Livin' on a Prayer" reminds me of every dance floor I've ever embarrassed myself on with friends. It makes me feel hopeful that Tommy and Gina made it after all.

"Landslide" reminds me of getting sober. It makes me feel kind of panicked for some reason.

"The House That Built Me" reminds me of my childhood home, the big front yard with the apple trees, the carport we'd sit under during storms, singing while my dad played the guitar. It makes me feel very, very sad.

Good music can help you connect with your emotions. What are the songs that make you Feel It All? Return to your achy, happy, sad, fiery playlist when you need to practice feeling your feelings.

.... reminds me of ....

and makes me feel ....

.... reminds me of ....

and makes me feel ....

.... reminds me of ....

and makes me feel ....

.... reminds me of ....

and makes me feel ....

.... reminds me of ....

and makes me feel ....

.... reminds me of ....

and makes me feel ....

.... reminds me of ....

and makes me feel ....

.... reminds me of ....

and makes me feel ....

.... reminds me of ....

and makes me feel ....

.... reminds me of ....

and makes me feel ....

How else might you practice Feeling It All?

1

2

3

4

5

FEEL IT ALL, USE IT ALL

TAMED

Sensitive is weak and overly emotional.

SENSITIVE

Sensitive is a superpower—
a capacity to feel deeply.

UNTAMED

"Tish is sensitive, and that is her superpower. The opposite of sensitive is not brave. It's not brave to refuse to pay attention, to refuse to notice, to refuse to feel and know and imagine. The opposite of sensitive is insensitive, and that's no badge of honor. In most cultures, folks like Tish are identified early, set apart, and considered eccentric but critical to the survival of the group. They are able to hear things others don't hear and see things others don't see and feel things others don't feel. The culture depends on the sensitivity of a few, because nothing can be healed if it's not sensed first."

What are you most sensitive about?

Who are some of the most sensitive people in your life?

What are some gifts that sensitive people bring to your life, relationships, and world?

....

....

....

....

....

....

....

What gifts does your sensitivity bring to your life, relationships, and world?

....

....

....

....

....

....

....

"What I thought would kill me, didn't. Every time I said to myself: *I can't take this anymore*—I was wrong. The truth was that I could and did take it all—and I kept surviving. Surviving again and again made me less afraid of myself, of other people, of life. I learned that I'd never be free from pain, but I could be free from the fear of pain, and that was enough."

Practice the process of thinking about your feelings as self-revelations. Make a list of five feelings you have experienced recently. Describe what each might reveal to you about you.

1

2

3

4

5

I have an Up Self who loves my life and a Down Self who doesn't. When I am my Down Self I forget all the good. So my Up Self wrote a note to my Down Self to help her remember.

When everything is terrible and I hate my life and I feel certain that I need a new career, a new religion, a new house, a new life, I look at my note from my Up Self and remember the good.

Write yourself a note about all the good in your life, relationships, and world. Return to it when you forget.

"When I pose a question about my life—in words or abstract images—I sense a nudge. The nudge guides me toward the next right thing, and then, when I silently acknowledge the nudge, it fills me. The Knowing feels like warm liquid gold filling my veins and solidifying just enough to make me feel steady, certain."

BE STILL AND KNOW

We spend all of our time, energy, words, and money creating a flurry, making sure that the snow doesn't settle so we never have to face the fiery truth inside us—solid and unmoving.

We keep ourselves shaken up
because there are dragons at our center.

What ways do you create a flurry to avoid being still, to not know what you know, to avoid seeing the dragons at the center of your life, relationships, and world?

1

2

3

4

5

"I came across a poem called 'A Secret Life,' about secrets and how we all have them.

I thought: *Well, I haven't had one since I got sober. I don't keep secrets anymore.* That felt good.

But then I read: 'It's what radiates and what can hurt if you get too close to it.'

I stopped reading and thought: *Oh, wait. There's one thing.*"

"My secret that radiates is that I find women infinitely more compelling and attractive than men. My secret is my suspicion that I was made to make love to a woman and cuddle with a woman and rely on a woman and live and die with a woman. Then I thought: *So odd. That cannot be real. You've got a husband and three children. Your life is more than good enough.*

I told myself: *Maybe in a different life.* Isn't that interesting? As if I had more than one."

What is a dragon at the center of your life that you are pretending not to see?

_____

_____

_____

_____

_____

_____

_____

_____

_____

_____

_____

_____

_____

_____

_____

What are the dragons at the center of your primary relationships?

What are the dragons at the center of your family, workplace, and community?

What are the dragons at the center of your nation and the world?

"When the things we use to keep the snow swirling—work, overscheduling, consumerism—are taken from us, we are forced to face the dragons of our lives, relationships, and nations."

"This forced settling is overwhelming, but it's also an opportunity—an opportunity for us to make changes in our lives and our communities."

Pick a dragon. Without committing to anything, what is a first step you might take to face it?

....

....

....

....

....

....

....

....

....

BE STILL AND KNOW

"It's my daily reminder that I always know what to do. That the answers are never out there. They are as close as my breath and as steady as my heartbeat. All I have to do is stop flailing, sink below the surface, and feel for the nudge and the gold. Then I have to trust it, no matter how illogical or scary the next right thing seems. Because the more consistently, bravely, and precisely I follow the inner Knowing, the more precise and beautiful my outer life becomes."

"I know many people who have
found this level inside them and live
solely by it. Some refer to the Knowing
as God or wisdom or intuition or source
or deepest self. I have a friend with
some serious God issues, and she calls it
Sebastian. A God by any other name
is an equal miracle and relief. It doesn't
matter what we call our Knowing.
What matters—if we want to live our
singular shooting star of a life—
is *that* we call it."

WE MUST BE STILL.

BAD NEWS:

When we're still, our dragons appear.

GOOD NEWS:

So does our intuition.

Intuition is the guide that helps us
slay our dragons.

Describe a time when you denied or defied your inner voice or Knowing. Why did you do it?

How did you feel when you made that decision against your Knowing?

What was the outcome?

Is there any way to honor that Knowing now? How might you course correct that decision?

I stand at the door and peek inside at my kids and their friends. The boys are draped all over the couch, and the girls are sitting in tiny, tidy, roly-poly piles on the floor. My young daughters are perched at the feet of the older girls, quietly worshipping.

My son looks over at me and half smiles. "Hi, Mom."

I need an excuse to be there, so I ask, "Anybody hungry?"

What comes next seems to unfold in slow motion.

Every single boy keeps his eyes on the TV and says, "YES!"

The girls are silent at first. Then each girl diverts her eyes from the television screen and scans the faces of the other girls. Each looks to a friend's face to discover if she herself is hungry. Some kind of telepathy is happening among them. They are polling. They are gathering consensus, permission, or denial.

Somehow the collective silently appoints a French-braided, freckle-nosed spokesgirl.

She looks away from the faces of her friends and over at me. She smiles politely and says, "We're fine, thank you."

The boys checked inside themselves. The girls checked outside themselves.

"We forgot how to know when we learned how to please."

If you stop doing, you'll start Knowing. We need to practice being still to get back in touch with our intuition. Close your eyes in a quiet place for ten minutes. Open your eyes. Describe your experience.

"At first, each ten-minute session felt ten hours long. I checked my phone every few moments, hoping my time was up. I planned my grocery lists and mentally redecorated my living room. The only things I seemed to 'know' on that floor were that I was hungry and itchy and suddenly desperate to fold laundry and reorganize my pantry. I was an input junkie thrown into detox. I was tempted to quit every second, but I was stern with myself: Ten minutes a day is not too long to spend finding yourself, Glennon. For God's sake, you spend eighty minutes a day finding your keys."

MOMENT OF UNCERTAINTY ARISES.

▽

BREATHE, TURN INWARD, SINK.

▽

FEEL AROUND FOR THE KNOWING.

▽

DO THE NEXT THING IT NUDGES YOU TOWARD.

▽

LET IT STAND. (DON'T EXPLAIN.)

▽

REPEAT FOREVER.

FOR THE REST OF YOUR LIFE:

Continue to shorten the gap between the Knowing and the doing.

Describe a time you honored your intuition/Knowing.

What gave you the courage to do so?

How did it feel to honor your Knowing?

....

....

....

....

....

....

....

What was the outcome?

....

....

....

....

....

....

....

....

"I understand now that no one else in the world knows what I should do. The experts don't know— the ministers, the therapists, the magazines, the authors, my parents, my friends, they don't know. Not even the folks who love me the most. Because no one has ever lived or will ever live this life I am attempting to live, with my gifts and challenges and past and people."

Is there a decision you need to make? Turn inward and sink. Feel for your Knowing. Is it nudging you toward one direction or another?

TAMED

Brave is being afraid and doing it anyway.

BRAVE

Brave is honoring your Knowing.

UNTAMED

"The braver
I am,
the luckier
I get."

"Brave does not mean feeling afraid and doing it anyway. Brave means living from the inside out. Brave means, in every uncertain moment, turning inward, feeling for the Knowing, and speaking it out loud. Since the Knowing is specific, personal, and ever changing, so is brave. Whether you are brave or not cannot be judged by people on the outside. Sometimes being brave requires letting the crowd think you're a coward. Sometimes being brave means letting everyone down but yourself."

When have you made a decision that defied expectations that your family, your community, your workplace, or the world had of you?

"Brave parenting is listening to the Knowing—ours and our children's. It's doing what's true and beautiful for our child no matter how countercultural it seems. It's about how when we know what our children need, we don't pretend not to know."

When have you made a decision for your child or someone you care for that honored your Knowing but defied the crowd?

"We must begin to live not from our indoctrination but from our imagination. Our minds are excuse makers; our imaginations are storytellers. So instead of asking ourselves what's right or wrong, we must ask ourselves: *What is true and beautiful?* Then our imagination rises inside us, thanks us for finally consulting it after all these years, and tells us a story."

DARE TO IMAGINE

Every life is an unprecedented experiment. This life is mine alone. So I have stopped asking people for directions to places they've never been. There is no map. We are all pioneers.

I wished I could ask Tabitha, "What's happening inside you right now?" I knew what she'd tell me. She'd say, "Something's off about my life. I feel restless and frustrated. I have this hunch that everything was supposed to be more beautiful than this. I imagine fenceless, wide-open savannas. I want to run and hunt and kill. I want to sleep under an ink-black, silent sky filled with stars. It's all so real I can taste it." Perhaps for us, as for Tabitha, the deepest truth is not what we can see but what we can imagine. Perhaps imagination is not where we go to escape reality but where we go to remember it.

"Women believe that
if we can imagine more,
it's because we're not
grateful enough—
instead of considering
that if we can imagine
more, it might mean
that we were made
for more."

Sketch the truest, most beautiful life you can imagine.

MY TRUEST, MOST BEAUTIFUL LIFE

"Women have sent me so many of their imaginings over the years. They say: 'For me, the truest, most beautiful life, family, world looks like. . . .' I marvel at how wildly different each of these stories is. It's proof that our lives were never meant to be cookie-cutter, culturally constructed carbon copies of some ideal."

Sketch something that represents the truest, most beautiful relationship you can imagine.

MY TRUEST, MOST BEAUTIFUL RELATIONSHIP

"A broken family is a family in which any member must break herself into pieces to fit in. A whole family is one in which each member can bring her full self to the table knowing that she will always be both held and free."

Write your vision for the truest, most beautiful family you can imagine.

"There is no one way to live, love, raise children, arrange a family, run a school, a community, a nation. The norms were created by somebody, and each of us is somebody. We can make our own normal. We can throw out all the rules and write our own. We can build our lives from the inside out. We can stop asking what the world wants from us and instead ask ourselves what we want for our world. We can stop looking at what's in front of us long enough to discover what's inside us. We can remember and unleash the life-changing, relationship-changing, world-changing power of our own imagination."

Describe the truest, most beautiful world you can imagine.

"The people who build their truest, most beautiful lives usually put pen to paper. It's hard to jump from dreaming to doing. As every architect or designer knows, there is a critical step between vision and reality. Before imagination becomes three-dimensional, it usually needs to become two-dimensional. It's as though the unseen order needs to come to life one dimension at a time."

How do your truest, most beautiful life, relationships, family, and world differ from your current life, relationships, family, and world?

DARE TO IMAGINE

"I want us all to grow so comfortable in our own feelings, our own Knowing, our own imagination that we become more committed to our own joy, freedom, and integrity than we are to manipulating what others think of us. I want us to refuse to betray ourselves. Because what the world needs right now in order to evolve is to watch one woman at a time live her truest, most beautiful life without asking for permission or offering explanation."

What are five things you want to do or have but have not allowed yourself?

1

2

3

4

5

DARE TO IMAGINE

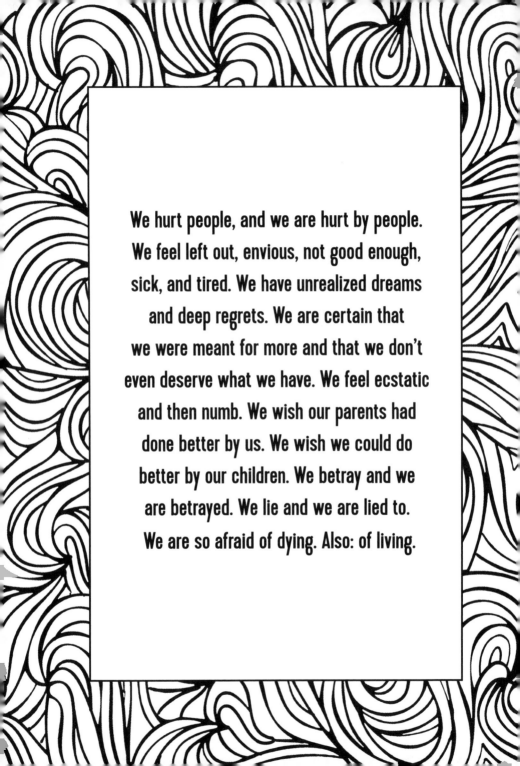

We hurt people, and we are hurt by people.
We feel left out, envious, not good enough,
sick, and tired. We have unrealized dreams
and deep regrets. We are certain that
we were meant for more and that we don't
even deserve what we have. We feel ecstatic
and then numb. We wish our parents had
done better by us. We wish we could do
better by our children. We betray and we
are betrayed. We lie and we are lied to.
We are so afraid of dying. Also: of living.

We have fallen in love and out of love, and people have fallen in love and out of love with us. We love our children, we long for children, we do not want children. We are at war with our bodies, our minds, our souls. We are at war with one another. We wish we'd said all those things while they were still here. They're still here, and we're still not saying those things. We know we won't. We don't understand ourselves. We don't understand why we hurt those we love. We want to be forgiven. We cannot forgive. We are lonely. We want to be left alone. We want to belong.

WE WANT TO BE LOVED.
WE WANT TO BE LOVED.
WE WANT TO BE LOVED.

Imagine a tough conversation that you need to have with someone. What are the things you need to say?

I need to get brave enough to talk to my dad about why we stopped communicating deeply. I'm writing this here so maybe one day I'll actually do it.

GET UNTAMED

GLENNON

"The truest, most beautiful life never promises to be an easy one. We need to let go of the lie that it's supposed to be."

"The blueprints of heaven
are etched in the deep desires
of women. What women want
is good. What women want
is beautiful. And what women
want is dangerous, but not
to women. Not to the common
good. What women want is a
threat to the injustice of the
status quo. The longings of
women should be the entire
world's marching orders."

TRUST YOURSELF

I have spent the last decade of my life listening to women talk about what they most desire. This is what women tell me they want:

I want a minute to take a deep breath.

I want rest, peace, passion.

I want good food and true, wild, intimate sex.

I want relationships with no lies.

I want to be comfortable in my own skin.

I want to be seen, to be loved.

I want joy and safety for my children and for all children.

I want justice for all. I want help, community, connection.

I want to be forgiven, and I want to finally forgive.

I want enough money and power to stop feeling afraid.

I want to find my purpose down here and live it out fully.

I want to look at the people in my life and really see them and love them.

I want to look at the news and see less pain, more love.

I want to look in the mirror and really see myself and love myself.

I want to feel alive.

What do you want?

I want ....

....

I want ....

....

I want ....

....

I want ....

....

I want ....

....

I want ....

....

I want ....

....

I want ....

....

I want ....

....

I want ....

....

TRUST YOURSELF

"Our deep desires are wise, true, beautiful, and things we can grant ourselves without abandoning our Knowing. Following our deep desire always returns us to integrity. If your desire feels wrong to you: Go deeper. You can trust yourself. You just have to get low enough.

So, a nightly desire for a bottle of wine? If your Knowing doesn't trust it, it's just a surface desire. A surface desire is one that conflicts with our Knowing.

We must ask of our surface desires: What is the desire beneath this desire? Is it rest? Is it peace?"

Write down a surface desire that you do not trust. What might be the deep desire beneath it that can be trusted?

....

....

....

....

....

....

....

....

....

....

....

....

....

....

....

....

....

....

TRUST YOURSELF

What are some things you have denied yourself because they do not fit with others' expectations?

Look back at your "I want" list. If you considered this list to be your marching orders, what might you do next?

"Your body will tell you things your mind will talk you out of. Your body is telling you what direction life is in. Try trusting it. Turn away from what feels cold. Go toward what feels warm."

What relationships in your life feel warm right now? Can you describe why?

What relationships feel cold? Can you describe why?

"These days, in business meetings, when I request an explanation for a decision someone has made, the women on my team know that I'm not looking for justifications, judgments, or opinions. I'm looking for knowing. So the decision maker will say, 'This option felt warm to me,' or 'partnering with them felt cold.' That will be the end of the discussion. I trust women who trust themselves."

"I am beginning to unlearn what I used to believe about control and love. Now I think that maybe control is not love. I think that control might actually be the opposite of love, because control leaves no room for trust—and maybe love without trust is not love at all. I am beginning to play with the idea that love is trusting that other people Feel, Know, and Imagine, too. Maybe love is respecting what your people feel, trusting that they know, and believing that they have their own unseen order for their lives pressing through their own skin."

List the people and things in your life that you try to control and the people and things that you trust.

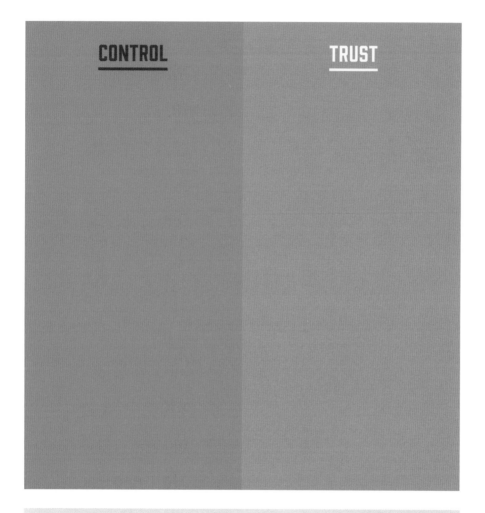

CONTROL

TRUST

When I did this exercise, every single thing and person in my life—including myself—was on the control side. Good times.

GLENNON

TRUST YOURSELF

Choose one thing or person from your control list. If you decided to trust instead of control, how would your approach to this thing or person change?

How might your own life change?

INTEGRITY

"Integrity means having only one self. Dividing into two selves—the shown self and the hidden self—that is brokenness, so I do whatever it takes to stay whole. I do not adjust myself to please the world. I am myself wherever I am, and I let the world adjust."

Do you ever feel like you have two selves—an outer self and an inner self? Describe how that feels.

Write about a time when your outer words and actions were not aligned with your inner self. How did this make you feel?

What were the outer and inner consequences?

....

....

....

....

....

....

....

....

....

....

....

....

....

....

....

....

....

....

GET UNTAMED

"Every time you're given a choice between disappointing someone else and disappointing yourself, your duty is to disappoint that someone else. Your job, throughout your entire life, is to disappoint as many people as necessary in order to avoid disappointing yourself."

Describe a time when you decided to disappoint yourself instead of disappointing someone else. What was the ultimate outcome?

Describe a time when you disappointed someone else instead of disappointing yourself. What was the ultimate outcome?

Who have you, throughout your life or right now, been most focused on pleasing?

What has pleasing these people cost you?

Fill in the spaces below.

WHO I need to disappoint next: ....

....

....

....

....

....

IDEAL I need to disappoint next: ....

....

....

....

....

....

EXPECTATION I need to disappoint next: ....

....

....

....

....

....

"Selfless women make for an efficient society but not a beautiful, true, or just one. When women lose themselves, the world loses its way. We do not need any more selfless women. What we need right now is more women who are full of themselves. A woman who is full of only herself no longer internalizes the world's memos and expectations. A woman who is full of herself knows and trusts herself enough to say and do what must be done, and lets the rest burn."

"Chaos is essential to creation.
Destruction is essential to
construction. If we want
to build the new, we must
be willing to let the old burn.
We must be committed
to holding on to nothing but
the truth. If truth can burn
a belief, a family, a business,
a religion, an industry—
it should have become
ashes yesterday."

LET
IT
BURN

"For a long while I contorted myself to live according to a set of old memos I'd been issued throughout my life about how to be a successful woman, mother, and Christian. I thought those memos were universal Truth, so I abandoned myself to honor them without even unearthing and examining them. When I finally pulled them out of my subconscious and looked hard at them, I learned that these memos had never been Truth at all— just my particular culture's arbitrary expectations. Hustling to comply with my culture's memos, I was flying on autopilot, routed to a destination where I wasn't even sure I wanted to land. So I took back the wheel. I quit abandoning myself to honor those memos. I abandoned the memos and began honoring myself. I began to live as a woman who had thrown away all the world's memos and wrote her own."

What ideals about what makes a good wife/husband/partner are you willing to let burn?

LET IT BURN

"I burned the memo that responsible motherhood is martyrdom. I decided that the call of motherhood is becoming a model, not a martyr. I unbecame a mother slowly dying in her children's name and became a responsible mother: one who shows her children how to be fully alive."

What ideals about what makes a good mother/parent are you willing to let burn?

LET IT BURN

"Every time my daughter looks at me,
she is seeing herself, too. And she is asking:

Mom, how does a woman wear her hair?
Mom, how does a woman love and be loved?
Mom, how does a woman live?

She is looking at me not as her hero but as
her model. She doesn't need me to save her;
she needs to watch me save myself."

Write your new memo about what makes a good mother/parent.

a Good Mother/Parent...

Me

LET IT BURN

She offered a new friendship memo: that for us there would be no arbitrary rules, obligations, or expectations. We would not owe each other anything other than admiration, respect, love—and that was all done already. We became friends.

She sent along this poem:

I honor your gods,
I drink at your well,
I bring an undefended heart
to our meeting place.
I have no cherished outcomes,
I will not negotiate by withholding,
I am not subject to disappointment.

Write your new friendship memo.

A Good Friendship...

Me

"Gender is not wild, it's prescribed. When we say, 'Girls are nurturing and boys are ambitious. Girls are soft and boys are tough. Girls are emotional and boys are stoic,' we are not telling truths, we are sharing beliefs—beliefs that have become mandates. If these statements seem true, it's because everyone has been so well programmed. Human qualities are not gendered. What is gendered is permission to express certain traits."

What are some gender ideas that you are willing to let burn?

What are some new gender ideas you might add to your memo?

"Our boys are born
with great potential
for nurturing, caring,
loving, and serving.
Let's stop training
it out of them."

In what ways will your new gender memo influence how you think about and interact with people who identify as boy/man?

LET IT BURN

In what ways will your new gender memo influence how you think about and interact with people who identify as girl/woman?

In what ways will your new gender memo influence how you think about and interact with people who identify as nonbinary, transgender, or gender expansive?

LET IT BURN

"Maybe we can stop trying so hard to understand the gorgeous mystery of sexuality. Instead, we can just listen to ourselves and each other with curiosity and love, and without fear. We can just let people be who they are and we can believe that the freer each person is, the better we all are. Maybe our understanding of sexuality can become as fluid as sexuality itself."

What are some ideas about sexuality that you are willing to let burn?

....

....

....

....

....

....

....

....

What are some new ideas about sexuality that you might add to your memo?

....

....

....

....

....

....

....

....

LET IT BURN

"Old leadership ideals have left far too many out for far too long because we've been conditioned to assume that the loudest, most opinionated, and most domineering people are the natural leaders. I have found that the opposite is true. To me, good leaders don't walk into a room and say: *Here I am!* They walk in and say: *There you are.* Strong leaders aren't those who shut others down with their bravado—but those who draw others out with their curiosity. The best leaders don't dominate conversations, they curate conversations. I've noticed that the quiet one in the room is often the best leader."

Write your new memo about what makes a good leader.

A Good Leader...

Me

LET IT BURN

Imagine that you actually are the leader of your life, relationships, family, and community. What is the first thing you would let burn?

....

....

....

....

....

....

....

What is the first new thing you would build?

....

....

....

....

....

....

....

....

....

"Often the internal voice telling us who God is and what God approves of is not God, it's our indoctrination. It's an echo of the voice of a teacher, a parent, a preacher— someone who has claimed to represent God to us. Many of those people have been well meaning, and others have only sought to control us. Either way, not a single one of them has been God's appointed spokesperson. Not a single one of them has more God in her than you do. There is no church that owns God. There is no religion that owns God. There are no gatekeepers. None of this is that easy. There is no outsourcing your faith. There is just you and God. Some of the hardest and most important work of our lives is learning to separate the voices of teachers from wisdom, propaganda from truth, fear from love, and in this case: the voices of God's self-appointed representatives from the voice of God, Herself."

"The God memos we get as kids are carved into our hearts. They are hard as hell to buff out. Everybody owes it to herself, to her people, to the world, to examine what she's been taught to believe, especially if she's going to choose beliefs that condemn others."

What is an idea about faith and religion you are willing to let burn?

....

....

....

....

....

....

....

....

What is an idea about spirituality or faith that you might add to your memo?

....

....

....

....

....

....

....

....

LET IT BURN

"I have lost identities, beliefs, and relationships it has hurt to lose. I have learned that when I live from my feelings, knowing, and imagination, I am always losing. What I lose is always what is no longer true enough so that I can take full hold of what is."

What identities, beliefs, and relationships in your life are no longer true enough?

1

2

3

4

5

LET IT BURN

"The memos I've written for myself are neither right nor wrong, they are just mine. They're written in sand, so that I can revise them whenever I feel, know, imagine a truer, more beautiful idea for myself. I'll be revising them until I take my last breath."

VOW OF THE BRAVE

If you keep living with integrity, the rest of your life will unfold exactly as it should. It won't always be comfortable. Some will recognize your brave, others won't. Some will understand and like you, others won't. But the way others respond to your integrity is not your business. Your business is to stay loyal to you. That way, you will always know that those who do like and love you are really your people. You'll never be forced to hide or act in order to keep people if you don't hide or act to get them.

"If we feel, know, and imagine—our lives, families, and world become truer versions of themselves. Eventually. But at first it's very scary. Because once we feel, know, and dare to imagine more for ourselves, we cannot unfeel, unknow, or unimagine. There is no going back."

BUILD
THE
NEW

When Abby and I fell in love, people had big feelings about our news. Sometimes their responses made me feel afraid, defensive, angry, too exposed.

One night, Abby said: "Glennon, I want us to think of our love as an island. On our island is you, me, the kids—and real love. The kind of love that novels are written about and people spend lifetimes trying to find. The holy grail. The most precious thing. *The* thing. We have it. It's still young and new, so we're going to protect it. Imagine that we've surrounded our island with a moat filled with alligators. We will not lower the drawbridge to let anyone's fear onto our island. On our island is only us and love. Leave anything else on the other side of the moat. Over there, it can't hurt us. We're here, happy on our island. Let them scream fear or hate, whatever. We can't even hear it. Too much music. Only love in, babe."

Sit down and decide with honor and intention what you will have on your island and what you will not. Not *who* your nonnegotiables are but *what* they are. Do not lower the drawbridge for anything other than what you have decided is permitted on your island, no matter who is carrying it. Understand that it is not your duty to convince everyone on your island to accept and respect you. It is your duty to allow onto your island only those who *already do* and who will walk across the drawbridge as the beloved, respectful *guests* they are.

Only Love In. Only Love Out.

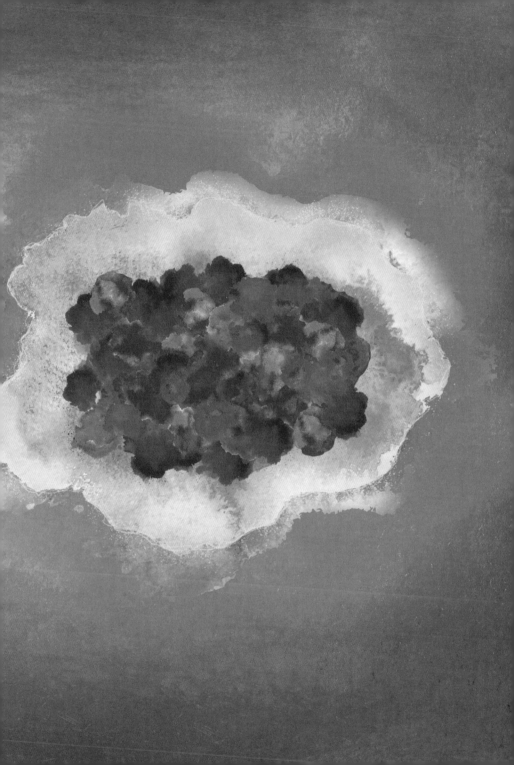

What will you not lower your drawbridge for? What are your nonnegotiables?

1

_____

2

_____

3

_____

4

_____

5

_____

GET UNTAMED

"When you are ready
to come to our island
with nothing but wild
acceptance and joy
and celebration for our
true, beautiful family,
we'll lower the
drawbridge for you.
But not one second
sooner."

What is currently on your island that needs to be removed?

....

....

....

....

....

....

....

What will you do next to remove from your island what does not belong there?

....

....

....

....

....

....

....

Sketch your truest, most beautiful island.

MY ISLAND

What is one thing you will do in order to build your truest, most beautiful life?

What is one thing you will stop doing in order to build your truest, most beautiful life?

Describe something you have always wanted that you plan to let yourself have.

Describe when and how you will practice Being Still each day.

"Abby is always asking me: 'What do you do for fun?' I find the question aggressive. What is fun? I don't do fun. I am a grown-up. I do family, work, and trash TV. Repeat forever. Why does she get to have fun? Who has the time and money for fun? I'll tell you who: everyone in this family but me. Craig has soccer and Chase has photography and the girls have ... everything. Everyone has a thing but me. Must be nice to have time for a thing. This *must be nice* thought stops me. It always does. Hmm. Maybe it is nice. Maybe that's why they all want a thing. Maybe I want a thing."

"I got myself a thing: playing guitar. It's hard, but it opens up another part of me, one that makes me feel more human. I think the word for this experience might be *fun*. But to have that fun, I had to climb down from Martyrdom Mountain. I had to allow myself one less thing to sigh about. I had to ask for help. I had to sacrifice some of my moral high ground, perhaps lose a few points in the She Who Suffers Most, Wins competition. I think we are only bitter about other people's joy in direct proportion to our commitment to keep joy from ourselves. The more often I do things I want to do, the less bitter I am at people for doing what they want to do."

List ten things that you like (or think you might like) to spend your time doing—small things or big things, just for you, just for fun.

1

2

3

4

5

6

7

8

9

10

BEAUTIFUL

"*Beautiful* means 'full of beauty.' Beautiful is not about how you look on the outside. Beautiful is about what you're made of. Beautiful people spend time discovering what their idea of beauty on this earth is. They know themselves well enough to know what they love, and they love themselves enough to fill up with a little of their particular kind of beauty each day."

Write about someone or something that filled you up with beauty recently.

"Hard work is important. So are play and nonproductivity. My worth is tied not to my productivity but to my existence. I am worthy of rest."

List ten things that you plan to do that will rest your body and restore your mind.

1

2

3

4

5

6

7

8

9

10

"Being human is not hard because you're doing it wrong, it's hard because you're doing it right. You will never change the fact that being human is hard, so you must change your idea that it was ever supposed to be easy. I will not call myself broken, flawed, or imperfect anymore.

Allow me to rewrite my own self-description:

I am forty-five years old.
With all my chin hairs and pain and contradictions, I am flawless, unbroken.
There is no other way."

Rewrite your own self-description.

I AM ....

....

I AM ....

....

I AM ....

....

I AM ....

....

I AM ....

....

I AM ....

....

I AM ....

....

BUILD THE NEW

"I am a human being, meant to be in perpetual becoming. If I am living bravely, my entire life will become a million deaths and rebirths. My goal is not to remain the same but to live in such a way that each day, year, moment, relationship, conversation, and crisis is the material I use to become a truer, more beautiful version of myself. The goal is to surrender, constantly, who I just was in order to become who this next moment calls me to be. I will not hold on to a single existing idea, opinion, identity, story, or relationship that keeps me from emerging freshly. I cannot hold too tightly to any riverbank. I must let go of the shore in order to travel deeper and see farther. Again and again and then again. Until the final death and rebirth. Right up until then."

Here's to the Untamed:

MAY WE KNOW THEM.
MAY WE RAISE THEM.
MAY WE LOVE THEM.
MAY WE READ THEM.
MAY WE ELECT THEM.
MAY WE BE THEM.

GLENNON DOYLE is the author of
the #1 *Sunday Times and New York Times*
bestseller *Untamed*, a Reese's Book Club
selection, which has sold over two million
copies worldwide. She is also the author
of the #1 *New York Times* bestseller *Love
Warrior*, an Oprah's Book Club selection, and
Carry On, Warrior. An activist and "patron
saint of female empowerment" (*People*),
Glennon hosts the *We Can Do Hard Things*
podcast. She is the founder and president
of Together Rising, an all-women-led
non-profit organization that has
revolutionized grassroots philanthropy —
raising over $30 million for women, families
and children in crisis. Glennon lives in
California with her wife and three children.